WHEN YOUR FRIEND IS EXCITED

BY ALLAN MOREY

BLUE OWL
BOOKS

TIPS FOR CAREGIVERS

Social and emotional learning (SEL) helps children grow their self and social awareness. They will learn how to manage their emotions and foster empathy toward others. Lessons and support in SEL help children build relationship skills, establish positive habits in communication and cooperation, and make better decisions. By incorporating SEL in early reading, children will have the opportunity to explore different emotions, as well as learn ways to cope with theirs and those of others.

BEFORE READING

Tell the reader that excitement is an emotion everyone experiences.

Discuss: What causes you to get excited? How does your mind and body feel when you are excited?

AFTER READING

Talk to the reader about how to recognize when someone else is excited.

Discuss: How can you tell when a friend is excited? What can you do and say to support that friend and join in his or her excitement? How can you help calm down a friend who is overexcited?

SEL GOAL

Young students struggle to understand their own emotions, and it's even more difficult for them to recognize how someone else is feeling. Being able to spot clues in a friend's body language and actions will help improve their social awareness skills. Lead a discussion about how students feel when excited and what helps them calm down if they become too excited. By sharing this information with each other, students will learn how to communicate with a friend who is feeling excited.

TABLE OF CONTENTS

CHAPTER 1

RECOGNIZING EXCITEMENT

When we are excited, we look happy! We smile. Our eyes open wide.

We also show excitement with **body language**. We might clap or rub our hands together. Tim waves his arms around when his favorite team wins!

It can be hard to sit still when we are excited! Carl and Tina get to go on a field trip today. They are excited! They skip to school.

We might fidget, jump up and down, or feel **restless**. Excited people sometimes laugh or talk loudly or quickly.

Our bodies **react** to excitement, too. Flamingos are Megan's favorite animal. She gets to see them at the zoo today! She had a hard time sleeping last night.

Today, she feels like she has butterflies in her stomach. Her heart beats fast, and she breathes more quickly.

EXCITED OR ANXIOUS?

Excitement and **anxiety** feel very similar. Both make our hearts beat faster. Both can cause our stomachs to flutter. Both may make us feel **jittery**. But excitement is a happy feeling. We feel anxiety when we are worried or nervous.

CHAPTER 2

UNDERSTANDING EXCITEMENT

Excitement is a positive **emotion**. It is what we feel when we are incredibly happy. We get excited about different things. Mike's brother is excited because it's his birthday!

Lila is excited to see her best friend. Both are **joyous** moments! It can be hard to understand why someone else is excited. But think. How do you feel when you're excited? This can help you understand someone else's excitement.

For some, excitement is hard to control. Britt's group knows the answer. Britt gets overexcited. She raises her hand but blurts out the answer before the teacher calls on her.

ANTICIPATION

Anticipation is part of excitement. We feel it when we are looking forward to something. It could be the first day of school. It could be a birthday party. Thinking about these events causes us to feel excited!

CHAPTER 3

RESPONDING TO EXCITEMENT

It is fun to see friends happy and excited. It is a time to celebrate and feel happy for them! When a friend is excited, support him or her. This will help your friend enjoy the moment.

Notice when a friend learns a new skill. Tell him or her, "Great job!" Liv landed a jump today! Her friend gives her a high five.

It is fun to be excited for someone else! Zach's gym class has been practicing basketball. Zach finally scores a basket! Members of his class cheer for him. They don't worry if they missed their shots.

Excitement is a powerful emotion. It affects how we think and act. We can get **overeager**. Steven's little sister gets so excited that she skips his turn. Steven reminds her whose turn it is. He asks her to be **patient**.

WAYS TO JOIN IN

Before you join in the excitement, check your surroundings. If you are in class, yelling with excitement can be too loud. But on the playground, we can run, jump, and yell! We can be excited with our friends in different ways.

When friends are excited, be happy for them. When your sister gets a present she likes, tell her how great it is! Your friend is excited to get ice cream. Ask, "What flavor will you get?"

Excitement is fun to **express**. It is fun to share with others, too!

GOALS AND TOOLS

GROW WITH GOALS

Everyone gets excited for different reasons. How can you show it and join in it when your friends are excited?

Goal: Share your excitement! What is something you are excited about? Talk about it with a friend!

Goal: Get excited for something that will happen in the future! It is fun to have something to look forward to. Can you think of something fun coming up? How can you prepare for it?

Goal: Support your excited friend! Ask your friend what excites him or her most about something and how it feels.

WRITING REFLECTION

Write down the things that excite you.
Ask a friend to do the same.

1. Compare your lists. What things did you write down that were similar? Which were different?

2. For the things that were different, explain to your friend why you get excited about them. Ask your friend to do the same.

3. Then talk about the things you had in common. Do you get excited about them for the same reasons?

GLOSSARY

anticipation
The feeling of expecting something to happen and being prepared for it.

anxiety
A feeling of worry or fear.

body language
The gestures, movements, and mannerisms by which people communicate with others.

emotion
A feeling, such as happiness, anger, or sadness.

express
To show what you feel or think with words, writing, or actions.

jittery
Feeling nervous or unable to relax.

joyous
Happy or delightful.

overeager
Excessively interested or excited.

patient
Able to put up with problems and delays without getting angry or upset.

react
To behave in a particular way as a response to something that has happened.

restless
Unable to relax or be still because of excitement, anxiety, or boredom.

TO LEARN MORE

FACT SURFER

Finding more information is as easy as 1, 2, 3.

1. Go to www.factsurfer.com

2. Enter "**whenyourfriendisexcited**" into the search box.

3. Choose your cover to see a list of websites.

INDEX

Blue Owl Books are published by Jump!, 5357 Penn Avenue South, Minneapolis, MN 55419, www.jumplibrary.com

Library of Congress Cataloging-in-Publication Data
Names: Morey, Allan, author.
Title: When your friend is excited / by Allan Morey.
Description: Blue owl books | Minneapolis: Jump!, Inc., [2020] Series: You've got a friend
Includes index. | Audience: Ages 7–10. | Audience: Grades 2–3.
Identifiers: LCCN 2019038057 (print)
LCCN 2019038058 (ebook)
ISBN 9781645272113 (hardcover)
ISBN 9781645272120 (paperback)
ISBN 9781645272137 (ebook)
Subjects: LCSH: Elation–Juvenile literature. | Agitation (Psychology)–Juvenile literature. | Emotions in children–Juvenile literature.
Classification: LCC BF575.E4 M67 2020 (print)
LCC BF575.E4 (ebook) | DDC 646.7/6–dc23
LC record available at https://lccn.loc.gov/2019038057
LC ebook record available at https://lccn.loc.gov/2019038058

Editor: Susanne Bushman
Designer: Molly Ballanger

Photo Credits: MidoSemsem/Shutterstock, cover; VEERAPONG CHAPARUNGSRI/Shutterstock, 1; somethingway/iStock, 3; Aaron Amat/Shutterstock, 4; TheVisualsYouNeed/Shutterstock, 5; shironosov/iStock, 6–7; Asier Romero/Shutterstock, 8–9 (foreground); Trong Nguyen/Shutterstock, 8–9 (background); Apollofoto/Shutterstock, 10; Kerkez/iStock, 11; mediaphotos/iStock, 12–13; Lotus_studio/Shutterstock, 14 (left); naluwan/Shutterstock, 14 (right); BIGANDT.COM/Shutterstock, 15; monkeybusinessimages/iStock, 16–17; LightField Studios/Shutterstock, 18–19; Hero Images/Getty, 20–21.

Printed in the United States of America at Corporate Graphics in North Mankato, Minnesota.